Notes from a Shipwreck

to Sarah

Notes from a Shipwreck

Jessica Mookherjee

*with love
+ Respect
Jess x*

Nine
Arches
Press

Notes from a Shipwreck
Jessica Mookherjee

ISBN: 978-1-913437-48-0
eISBN: 978-1-913437-49-7

First published August 2022 by:

Nine Arches Press
Unit 14, Sir Frank Whittle Business Centre,
Great Central Way, Rugby.
CV21 3XH
United Kingdom

www.ninearchespress.com

Nine Arches Press is supported using public funding by Arts Council England.

Supported using public funding by
**ARTS COUNCIL
ENGLAND**

For my sisters

Contents

"Had I been any god of power, I would
have sunk the sea within the earth or ere
it should the good ship so have swallowed and
the fraughting souls within her."

   – *The Tempest (1.2.10)*

"Moaneth always my mind's lust
that I fare forth, that I afar hence
seek out a foreign fastness."

   – *The Seafarer (Translt. Pound)*

Notes from a Shipwreck

We go whaling in the Violent Blue and the crew
are lit by sperm oil, perfumed by ambergris – our Nantucket
night-birds sing a parliament of beer-filled chants.
We wonder if the tales of monsters are real, details charted.
We tie the stove up in red-tape so it doesn't kill us.

The Captain asks me to cook Bengali fish and pray
to the Hindu sea god, Varuna, god of rain. Lightning strikes
us, I thought he knew where we were going? *Salus Populi*
he blusters in Latin, says he thinks he's packed enough
limes and lemons. I must stink wearing this foul plastic.

Her fluke takes us down – for the whole catastrophe
of things we did to her and the sea. I was just a ship-trapped
girl on a rock, far from homeland, it was nothing to do
with me, just a *bloody foreigner*. I watch as they harpoon her.
We wipe our sleeves while wreckers look on, light fires

on the shore. What a disaster the stink is for all the sailors
left. Next comes scurvy, next comes fever. The captain brings
us a remedy named after a baby whale who washed up
on the banks of the Thames, near Barnes Bridge, last summer.
I stood by when the crowds came to witness her carcass.

Flotsam

I'm changed into these rocks and am full of noises, a fox scream, badger scratch and twig snap in symphony of flesh instruments and I itch and hum until my ears sing. My voice is kelp as I wake. He calls me Miranda, says I'm his good, good girl, says my mother used me like a doll, discarded, broken and painted blue. I am unspoken, unseen and untaken. If only I could sink a sea; rich and strange. Vases shake when I'm around, he says. He'll make me sleep, never let me cross the wine-dark oceans and yet I know I can make creams and potions. I read his books, learn to open clouds and caves where he hides the secrets. I can turn him into frog, newt, fish and smear his pulped and pestled pages into my carved, fermenting skin.

Outcaste

I was no longer a Brahmin girl   the day I left on that boat with my mother
across the bay from Mumbles to Ilfracombe   I'd never seen the sea so hard like
salt dunes   *Are we in England now*? I asked   We used the Severn Bridge after
that   and I thought it was the Howrah Bridge   I was sick on my mother's
lap   They took me there after the war   They say: *I must not cross
the sea.*   My father called me *Badmash*   the day I stole his chequebook,
says I'm no Brahmin girl, no – even before that   when I took money from
her purse to buy my sisters Christmas presents   from the shops up the
road, wrapped toys up in cheap tissue paper and ribbons   told them they
were from Santa, rigged up bells   They say: *I must not steal*   *from a
Brahmin*   I was not a Brahmin girl when I told all the Welsh kids   at
school   I was from India, not England   They were eased   having
learned the sins of the English from their fathers   But in my heart   I knew
I was born in Luton   They say: *I must not bare false witness with respect   to
land*   The Dharmasutra says to become pure I must fast   for three
days, only take a small portion of food   For three days I must   bathe at
dawn, noon and dusk   I must stand all day, and sit all night   I have never
done these things   I am unruly, always standing and sitting   at the wrong
times and eating crisps   The Dharmasutra requires I do these   rituals for
three years in order to return home.

Truant

She's in and out of the bedroom, *saw-shark, minnow, silverfish*   too
small to get onto the top shelf   Smells all unfamiliar, suitcases
under the bed, the boast of carpet swirling like her mother on
medicine   The carpet, so damp underfoot, the sea from half
a mile down the lane seeps with fog into the house, nestled in
huddles in the heft and weft   Greens, reds, plucked in paisley,
stamps of mould growth, paint blistered and sticks in worn places
She strokes the book   A title she shouldn't understand, but she
does. Opens it up, illicit, she's cross-legged on a bedspread   She
shifts, turns pages, words penetrate   darts her eyes across a
gloaming room and the creak of stained wood   uncommitted
boards, heave of banister makes her ear cock to the small sounds
and she thumps the book back in its wicked place   What
does it matter what she did? *Robin, blackbird, sparrow, thrush.*

She asks if her lunch is ready, curls her nose at the sweat from
her mother's uncovered breasts   She creeps, watches paint
peel from the skirting boards, picks at it, bores a hole into the
future, watches herself tut-tut and weep   watches herself
become *mountain, river, cloud, rain, whale, rhinoceros, polar bear.*
Itches crevices, in her bedroom, cuts up books in her bedroom,
alone in her bedroom, walks around the house in her bedroom,
hears her mother's voices in her bedroom   She scratches her
thighs   in soft places made hard and scales cake over her, turn
her; *mackerel, crab, limpet*   In pours silence, between her legs,
in her bedroom   A dam burst of water cough floods through her
bedroom   Who keeps laughing?   Who is laughing
in this rain-soaked room?

/

A mother soaked in a language made of tongue twist, babbled voices blithering in a din from a blister-packed mouth   She is a chorus of birds, *parakeet, bulbul, shikra*   Alone in a bedroom, inside an Indian forest, stalking woman, dressed as tiger   tiger dressed as mother, crouching on all fours   aimed rear, pissing at your heart to scent mark   Owned by the dark she hides in a book, in the ones she's not to look at, in the ones she does   She creeps, sideways and up, sideways and up, every sense locked on the sound of a cough, a sneeze   a laugh that burbles up   Springs out of a bedroom, covered in leaves. Fur lined on the inside, she piles on her clothes   a substrate of rags   in the silence of wood, in a groan of a house, where no one comes, where the dishes get done, where food is wiped, where food is served, in suppressed boils of laughter   Who is laughing in the slab of the house?   She silently lines herself in the pages of books in her bedroom.

Plague Rounds

Blood. Write down a thousand times how we are plagued,
each day, a new lesson, correcting bitter herbs of past. Today
I spill things, feel gravity change, makes me appear
stronger than I am. Blood-being, thicker than it looks. Frogs

sit on my hand, cover me in embryos, in my state of eggs.
I feel my belly. Clock the boy in school, so proud
of his tiny prick; I pinch it, he says *let's get married* so I run
to the toilets, cry, *don't let me have to look after those million babies.*

I turn to locust. Learn tit-for-tat, tiger attack, I don't look
at blood-smash from dinner plates he hurls at her.
How she breaks as I'm left to eat, now I write *I'm not like her,*
write it a thousand times. I, with shaven head, *I must not lie*

down in the street with lice or in rooms with dogs. I itch-scratch
sores, lick dust from pores, bitten by unforgiving bursts,
hide under cervices, cracks under floors. I'm plague, the papers
say. I'm swarm, flooding and boils. On TV a father clutches

his baby daughter, her leg blown from a land mine, as he runs
over paddy fields to get her help. A camera follows him.
I'm an Indian mutiny. They're cattle and I'm a training vet.
Mother feeds me fish fingers, Father talks of nuclear threat.

He's in chemicals, blows it, *Abracadabra,* turns it plastic, boils,
chokes them into baby whales and cadavers. Now I recycle,
become vegan, write it out in hail a thousand times, build
shelter from discarded water bottles. I love the thunder;

this weird weird weather as I comb the shore for ambergris,
and cling to darkness to save me and my love of things. I write
out a thousand times how the dark is pregnant with what I've left.
At zero hour I watch your face, release you from the grasp.

This is how we spit out our lives and write the lines, again,
of how we were first born in the jetsam of burning ships,
wearing signs that say; *I'm not my mother, I'm not my mother*
and you're not your father, as we sing: *uncurse, uncurse, uncurse.*

Cracked Actors

That summer I became Puck, Miranda, Titania,
you turned Romeo, Ferdinand and Antonio.
Let's run away you said. *Peter Pan the fuck
out of here.* You stole your dad's Vauxhall Cavalier,
I stole my dad's chequebook, and we drank as you drove
down the motorway. I was in love with Bowie and you
were amused and jealous as I sang along to Diamond Dogs,
Sweet Thing and Five Years. You said I was beautiful
so I shaved off my eyebrows and spiked up my hair
and cupid-blind, I knew you were desperate. I stood
on the hotel room's bed with fishnets, a fake-fur jacket,
painted lips of dust-ruby to take you. In the mirror we melted
together. Show reel slow, *is it hunky dory*? I wanted to know.
The tape recorder we bought on the way played Lady
Stardust. We acted like movie stars. Nothing was safe.
You were slicked back, I waxed and waned, made up
from a strange thing of you. Someone clapped, did we
make it from the bones and blood of us? All smeared
like lipstick on the sheets as we fell to earth.
I was a vixen when I was back at school. You, Oberon,
had a line or too to get through. I was playing
kitchen sinks and gin until you were out of my system.

The Shipboard Girl

take a close look at that cheap girl who can look
expensive with a lipstick made in New Jersey
and the watery sun on her red lips is transformative
as her skincare routine but today it's out of the
window for she hopes the buoy is Jesus certain to
save her if she goes overboard as she's meeting
that talented young man she's longed for below
the deck *Oh John* she sighs *i love that you can
speak so many languages* and there's his scarf tied
around her bright hair that's the colour of the ship's
railings while the white sea turns her skin into salt

Gorgon

They are flushed, heat-ravaged and keeping cool
on the bus to the station from the airport.
He's as ripe and golden as unbitten fruit, a smile
half-moon, half-man. The curve of his thigh muscle
twitches next to her. She's a small brown hen, dun
coloured, a promise inside her not yet realised.
She adores him perhaps, moves her eyes and holds
herself away from him. They're silent but a lover's
language leaks out as he touches her thigh
and she melts, curves into his shape.
But then she stiffens, a silent barrier gives
way and she tenses her arm across her breasts.
He tightens his grip on her with long fingers
and I also fall in love with her – in her dun coloured
summer dress, her pale cream features
which will not hold age well.

I see them much later; she leads the way through
the Palazzio Dei Vecchio, her eyes on Perseus
as he holds up Medusa's head.

Caliban

Hidden under a shade as the heat peals layer after layer
of mesh, pins in his clothes, needles in his legs   Arms
thick of bones and boards he attaches a loop into his chest
in tension and twine he pulls taught   He pokes in
a dowel made of teeth and fixed sharp with points and
ends with a slip-knot   A terrific silence   He pulls
off the lark's head and stops the song caught in the hitch.

The Portent

One day he takes everything down, his beads and bangles. Slips off his face.
Says *nothing exists* as he sits with her in the moon's rays

and waits for the records to flip. One day she expects Comet West to appear,
from far north, shining, wild eyed, ready for the morning's electric blue sky.

One day she stays up all night to watch his dazzle, tail-spin and coma.
She sees him outgas, surpass himself as he unbuckles,

falls through leaves, flies to the horizon. Somewhere from a basement
he plays an instrument of rock dust, light pressure and water ice.

From earth, her eyes dart from side to side to follow his blaze. He doesn't see
her going cold, chart a course, find a map of space to point

where he goes, all crazed on the radio waves. One day she makes sense
of his punch-drunk songs as he flies too near the sun.

One day she might predict his return, burned out in a shower of meteorites.
One day she'll take everything down, naked eyes and records.

Eating with Hands

Through the thumb comes space / Through the forefinger comes air
Through the mid-finger comes fire / Through the ring finger comes water
Through the little finger comes earth

The knives and forks are gossiping about us as we silently put them in places out of harm's way. They notice the tiger and its too-big grin, barge in, know that it'll devour everything, so they sigh, lie flat dry and untouched by us in their sharp and shiny way, because the tiger's teeth are masters of severing. It prowls cupboards, goes through the bread bin, the fridge, barely glancing. Placing weight where we put the meanings of our rhymes, where we empty vast slop buckets as it pisses and catches its hair in every sharp corner with daily duties. They clatter and clink about us, say that man can't rouse his wife, or give those kids proper advice, just fights and bickers, pulls each implement out and argues about how to wash and sharpen them. They say the tiger doesn't need them. Knives and forks are cowards, unlike the teacups – fragile, held trembling between her fangs.

Black Water Shanty

after Rimbaud's The Drunken Boat

A sad-fired blood blows from her veins
a boat launched through age-opened sea

a flare gun launches a yell of shocks
unsteady, roll and loll, hit hard waves –

all those sick bursts hurtle weather into her
sad-fired blood blows from her veins
into a boat launched by age-opened sea

spit out churn, bile empties over stern
she holds on to a keening bow, as the crew

        sing   *where will she go? where will she go?*

spit out churn, bile empty over stern
she swallows morning-after pills

hangs over the side till she's all spat out
as a broken girl, churns, a lifeboat crew

sing   *give her a dose of salt and water*

they smash the sextant, throw over star-takers
a broken lifeboat turns shock waves and waters
she bursts tempests like her father taught her –

turns magic tricks learned from stranded books
a broken lifeboat churns the black waters as the crew

sing   *you don't know your way home*

Tethys

She's lost her diary. The one where she makes
plans for the future, where she creates order in the waters.
Her ex-husband, the Ocean, turned into a voice in her head:

> *I thought this place was an island,*
> *I thought you would bear fruit for me*
> *here, among the rocks…*

She thinks she's left it in the wardrobe. Mutters to herself,
she throws her clothes around the bedroom, shaves off
the sheet ice, scratching herself on stalactites.

She sits on her bed, heaped and crying out in a banishment
of whole chapters, stories happening without her.
She spies all the others laughing & drinking cocktails

from her lookout on the frozen moon of Saturn.
There is a small part of me left, a part that I own…
She remembers how she became reduced to permafrost.

The next man she meets, she will turn him
into a cormorant to save him from drowning, give him a metal beak
to sheer through her frozen skin.

Harpy

Just before I opened my eyes I knew how the marks
on my sister's arse were made. My dream made it clear.

This morning I've a dreadful hankering for all the parts
of a goddess – even her eggs. I will eat all of it.

I am suddenly afraid my feathers will fly away, that I will
not find any openings and my bones will snap.

I enjoy regurgitation, dislike the precision of sound, small
noises make me want to tear necks. I fear for the children

next door. Now I'm owl, free to despise, with no guilt
or shame, which is what I loathe about humans.

My only god is a feather, mostly skin, some call it sky.
I worship the accuracy that creates feathers. Storm swift,

the world becomes red, soon dark becomes fast, moans,
hom-hom. I become hot in sharpness, an unheard pitch.

I test these feathers, these vehicles; the soundless rip
that swallows life's meaning shrinks to the only living thing.

Sea Voices

I.

I was called Lascar by the sea. I stoked its blood vessels, made steam with my black scales.

II.

I was called Sepoy by Varuna, slapped by the temple master, numb to the roar I heard. Told to march in bare feet miles through jungle to the earth's end, for no reason other than to keep the Brahmin's secrets. No better than white masters. I was called Seaboy by the sea, salt air's my lover: I'm his open pore.

III.

In 1759 I was called Abdullah, one of the attendants of Mir Zafar and sent to the Majesty's court with the wild cat named Saugus, so wild it needed a constant companion. I fed it mice and sweet cakes, it called me Mister, had plans for me: said I could be the Lord Mayor of London, but the King sent me back across the Black Water. The sea called me again in 1764 as an attendant of a leopard called Bhag. The governor of Madras hoped to impress the King who, terrified, locked us both up in a Tower next to jewels from my homeland.

IV.

I was called by the sea. White Tara flowed into me. *Monk,* she whispered, *sail to where the rain lives and offer them peace.* I was called her lover. I built temples to her breasts in every island I worshiped.

V.

I was called indifferent by the sea, called Bay of Bengal. I was called the bite, sound, the end of the world.

When God Visits Me He's Covered in Glitter,

slippery, quiet in his mime costume,
with little to tell me; pretends to cry
at my sad fall downs, does the *trapped-
in-a-box* thing with his hands, pulls
on an invisible rope, hangs his head.
Sometimes Prospero, sometimes Miranda,
sometimes Ariel, can't always tell
if he tries to scare or soothe as prayers
are answered in cryptic clues
and dance moves. Whimsical, he turns up
as a woman clothed in glistening fish,
a bower bird or sharp-suited magpie,
whatever the mood, tells me things
in shrieks and spears a word or two my way,
cut up from magazines. He did fall to earth
in my dream once, dressed as a blue-jay
with a wide brimmed hat, told me secrets,
but I suspect he tells everyone, says *Satori*
is the answer and I know that's a trick
to keep me listening.

The Professor of Primates

For Volker Sommer

How far away he is from Reinhardswald,
those rich folded forests where Sleeping Beauty slept.
How his eye looks, attached as it is, to his aorta, breathes
with his valves and myths. He automatically clicks
computer buttons, unravels to his pupils,
how the swing of Lar, Hoolock, Siamang, respond
to their opera. And only the front row of his class know
his eyes become mist. A shaft of sun from the street
distracts his screen, a flicker of London Plane, disturbed
by windfall and squirrel, shadow-tails from a tree.

He will save those jungles with his body.
Gower Street, Darwin Building, stained walls of dust
and Latin, skulls and clavicles glow in strip-lit municipal,
dissected by metal blinds. And he can't teach this beauty,
but lets music of Khao Yai jungles be heard. They,
who are given numbers, with their impossible arms
and songs, are his friends. A girl at the back asks him how
can kindness evolve from chemicals. He repeats;
Altruism does not exist. The Lar don't sing for him.
And a tiger's hot breath on her face wakes her up again.

The Slip

To captain a ship of flesh is no mean feat; a trick
known by shadow and stars as sea-clocks tick. With a sperm
whale in your belly, the ocean is a blood-black overreach.

With pips in your guts, you bellow with men at the abort point.
You're old enough to know better. They call you Boy Wonder
with glinting eyes. *Where there are gulls, there are eggs,*

they cry. The land's full of grief-water.
The lubbers from the Hooghly murk across the slew
of the Trent, Ouse, Lea, and into the black water.

Worse things happen at sea, bitterlings, spawning coral.
The first crime's to get aboard the ship. Mother lets you go
with no temples, no plan. Navigate by moonlight,

read stars, taste wind, fall short, learn that dirty weep
of sore-tongue sailor-speak. Listen for the siren.
Fly-speck rations to peck on. Hardtack in cupboards.

From the warm and saline, a white bird lands
on deck. You bathe under its beady eye. No rhyme
or reason. You cut that mooncalf out on the quarterdeck,

leave it, dazed in its sea of gut-blood to the gull shriek,
crying its soul out. Slip the baby whale into the ocean
without rituals: *there she blows,* a shape in black water.

One Evening in November

I kept telling him a story of the bird held by that skipper when I was in Vancouver that time, a storm-petrel, no bigger than a sparrow, caught up in nets some weeks before. The skipper rescued it, fed it from sea-worn hands. I couldn't stop telling him, though a fragment of myself saw how he watched me speak about that gust-wailing day on the catamaran out to find the orca, those blustering tales had him shivering. I saw behind his eyes, how he'd known that storms can break a man, but I didn't think about that, I was telling him my story of the storm-petrel. The skipper kept it in a bath, called the bird *Pete*, fed it milk and a little bread, a few worms until it was strong for life, said it was a special day to set it free. We saw it go, push air over muscle, its heartbeat focused on the earth's pull. The skipper flung that creature no bigger than my palm to the sky. We raced far out as we could from shore, no going back; I kept saying these things as he shivered and closed the back door. I waved my hands in swooping gestures, as I told him how the bird pounded the air next to the boat. We cheered for the creature, I said, some of us were crying, hoping it would walk on water, the skipper even said, *watch Pete go,* and then the gulls; gunned terror with hungry yells and lunged as the bird darted and swerved in a fit for breath, more for life, a hunted Morse-code heartbeat. The skipper jibbed and boomed-jacked the hull for an hour, used the boat as a breast of armour. We watched as storm-loud gulls fed on the wing. I kept telling him these things.

Anchorage

It's almost like I was watching him. *Is it OK?* He says,
Fine, no problem, I like it, he shrugs and leaves.
I'd like to be an engineer like my father was.
Autumn falls from his hands, an instrument, a pen.

His hour struck me in dark-god purple, sun-rise pink,
says he's dying to get away, have something
to look forward to. We sit in silence as I try
the tea he's made for me, it's like holding a star

in my hands, makes me want to jump into water,
clean myself of what he's made me. He says
I've too many attachments, most of all to my body.
I suck all my knowledge of Hindu myth, tell him

perhaps you'll go to Valhalla after all. It's almost like
I was watching him. *Is it OK?* He says. *Fine,
No problem, I like it.* He shrugs and leaves.
The door bell strikes in my ears. John comes, late,

to the porch, shaking off the rain. I clean up after him,
mud trails through the house. He didn't want to come in,
hid out on the golf course for three nights, hungry,
though he didn't know it. Now he's a feral thing –

eats when he wants, learned to talk bit by bit. I say
*Let's watch that film we like, about Kasper Hauser,
I like the bit where he thinks apples are people.*
But he doesn't answer. I'd like to be an engineer,

just like my father was. Autumn falls
into his hands, an instrument, a pen. His hour
strikes me in dark-god purple, sun-rise pink. He says
I want to hold a star in my hand and jump into water.

He folds, unfolds hands in his lap, makes signs.
The blood gushes through my body in that moment,
as if I'm a gutter. And I know, in that moment, people
are in love with each other, carousing in a longhouse.

I sit with John, outside things, writing a letter.
I mumble, absent vowels, bitten consonants.
I'd like to be an engineer, like my father was,
autumn falls to his hands, an instrument, a pen.

I'd like to be an engineer just like my father was
and maybe end up in Valhalla after all, to amaze
the Hindu gods. John says perhaps he'll emerge
one day into sunlight, wondering who he is.

Jetsam

The size of my finger-tip, I displayed
it in my palm, cracked, blue speckled,
paper-thin. I took it to him –
covered in dew, my cheeks cold
with wet leaves. I asked *What is this?*
He put his paper down on the coffee table,
took his glasses off. An egg-fallen,
a bird-life cut, a halt of a mother's count.
She is upstairs talking to herself.
I read I was inside my grandmother once,
in a famine; felt pecking, a rise of seeds
and blood, a need to run into the world
and bury myself inside earth, in case I should
also crack, fall away, slip into air.

Jail Birds

The crow keeps records of my movements,
no need for locks, his beak is keen and fast.

Everywhere the starlings gather, they chitchat
everything, quick-quick. I go back to my cell

to get away. Each night they want me to eat
small mice, or snails, whatever the owls put

in front of me. They watch, heads turned. I say
it's good grub but I throw up. The owl is pleased,

I know this because her barn feathers get thick
and bright as my throat clogs. She doesn't speak.

I spend my time alone, in my cell, tearing up
pieces of paper. The birds think I'm nesting.

And the Harbourmaster Says

For centuries, friends; on our island nations,
Wars protected our people;
Shipwrights and engineers; men and women
Kept our fortunes floating.
Now in this post-Brexit world we are building
Daring aircraft carriers, frigates, destroyers,
Warships built by men and women.
Next, friends; two mighty flagships are coming;
Dreadnought submarines; Type 45 Destroyers;
And a phalanx of frigates – not just building
Type 26 Global Combat Ships.

and the ghosts say

when father died, men from Haverton yard came to tell me. so many shipwrecks
on this stretch of the coast. he'd no business to be out at sea in heavy weather,
we never saw him, he was barely a father. it was Arab John
from Furnesses' who ran up the hill that day to tell me my husband was dead.
at the door, a hand at my skirt and a kicking inside. a metal sheet fell on him,
and he was finished, just like that. barely had time to be a father,
and i took his overalls, washed grime off them, took them in at the waist
turned them up, wore them, and built the bloody ships myself. all the knots,
lugging, stitching, mending, making. i can still see John now, running up that hill.

And the Harbourmaster Says

Next, friends; there will be people, growing
On the Clyde, Forth, in Belfast, Barrow, Bute,
Shipyards supplying parts, from Rosyth to Appledore,
Portsmouth, Hebburn, and beyond.
We will continue to keep building
Certainty on the warships, matching
The feats of their forebears, tomorrow's engines
Of our future economic growth.

Dear J

I read my diary again today, to see if I mention you.
It is sparse. I looked for the entry on the day I decided to leave.
Losing your love feels like what happened with my mother;
a reflection of a torn polaroid, dark corners and cold,
barely holding, watching for unpredictable movements.
We were on a ship weren't we? I'd stolen some money
and that trip was horrible. Everyone was sick.
You told me things that would come true in the future.
There was little to keep us together. The sea is not glue.
I'd never find refuge again. Anyway, there isn't much
in the diary. Some lists of bills I needed to pay. I did find
something – years later, I wrote out a dream I had of you.
I was embarrassed because I'd heard from friends
you were doing so well, all settled and buying sofas.
And there I was dreaming about you. I don't know
why I decided to write it down. I keep a logbook,
only I know about it. I think we can be friends though, so many years
have passed. We are still both alive after all. Like a shipwreck;
covered in sea moss and worms. Alive despite ourselves.
There is always friendship on the shore. We learn
to construct from old timber, we perfect fires and foraging.
I find an old picture of you sitting next to a friend who didn't
make it. We look so young in those photographs.

Overboard

with Simon Tje Jones

One of our sailors is missing. The sky's stricken,
a torn timetable, as squall sets in.
The night before he leaves he wants to share.
I'm on scullery duty and turn away.

An empty chair at check-in, shorter queue
for meds. He hung around before the bend.
He's left his compass, dirt from his trousers,
blind spot near wires, and tunnelled into the drink.

He's just a boy full of wine-dark sea. I hold the bench
so as not to fall in, the last bitter end of rope, tune
into silent periods before helicopters come.
They ask us for information, spin his room,

pile sandbags to stop a storm, ask questions
about his appearance and state of mind – nobody
speaks. I keep his place, his phone number written
on my hand. One of our sailors is missing.

Hungry Ghost

Write prayers for the dead today, feed them rice balls.
They see only three children, say there is another one
somewhere, knocking on the outline of a womb. *Write
me a prayer*, feed them through their tiny throats filled
with air, can't write prayers for the dead these days,
they knock on my door with wild streaks, a sugar rush,
opening up, unbolting, unlocking the doors, fumbling
for keys. This is a thin time, skin is bursting, scratch my
feet, want to barefoot into the garden where the ghost
keeps looking for the lost child; *Come inside* whisper
the dead, *don't be angry*. I won't feed prayers to the dead,
I reply, they make demands to be fed sugared almonds,
want cow's milk, sixteen rice balls before the burn, want
me to change them into ether. *Must I feed these children
that don't exist?* They don't look into my eyes, *We are not
far away*, they say. Won't someone write a prayer to feed
me, that I might appear where that hunger lives?

Dazzle Ship

Into this bright zebra searchlight, I'm in camouflage
disrupting an empty ocean, heavy battleship marooned in a house.

I walk into a garden, where I'm greened with aphid. It's Sunday
and I'm on alert, sonar, radar will kill the noises in case

it gives me away. It's the sound of a washing machine, the wind,
a car alarm – insistent, broken-laughter green. The stupid light

is arched, it's hard to see. I'm dots and dashes, a repetition
of Morse code on your shoulder. You give me an old box camera,

show me the three fingers left on your rifle hand, as I stride out
with darkness on my face, hoping to be spotted on the horizon.

Ariadne and Theseus

She can't see
his faint tang of musk, smothered
in disinfectant and aftershave. A spray of perfume
to hide emissions of shame, he leaves windows
open to let his scent out, scrubs his skin.
She breathes in his shirt-stink, a pain dims.

He can't hear
her body against him. To get his bearings, twig
hurt underfoot, marks gouged in bark with fingernails
to find his way back to her in the dark. The rub
of rope-skein burnt on his hands, her trail of spider silk
unravelled, finding his feet, his blood reaching out.

Long Glass

i.   She's become detached   and sees her eyes fill up with glass.

ii.   when her mother looks away there is nothing but screaming for days and days.

iii.   he went blind when Gomorrah exploded   there was a lot of *pass the salt please would you dear* at the dinner table.

iv.   *don't keep scratching there*   *keep your legs together*   trying too hard to be teacher's pet   making everyone flinch.

v.   he stares from his position at the window hoping no one can see.

vi.   all the rooms inside his skull   arguing.

vii.   glass half full   half empty   half full   half empty it is easy to be optimistic when you are blind drunk.

viii.   *and she barged into the pub and smashed the optics*   *she totally lost it*   *the blokes looked up from their glasses and said* *'I   don't fancy yours much'.*

ix.   he never once thought about her until one day a quanta of a molecule escaped from his memory and he knew the colour of her eyes again.

x.   you might outgrow your stories   every single one you tell yourself you might stand in a thunderstorm naked and go where the rain goes.

xi.   the ophthalmologist's wife walks a dog made of tears around the block trying to escape her husband's demands.

xii.   she poked herself in the eye   made a hole in her skull   next to her pupil.

xiii.   then when she couldn't talk, she started crying in the hospital.

xiv.   the light is forced in for so long that you blister. Light is good in small doses.

The Storm

Cloud builds by a performance of droplets   moving circus
beasts eaten by the sky in a ring ripped from a finger   *Show us*
what you can do   Yesterday it was hard to hear your silence,
harder to whip into an emergency   You said *No*   *I can do*
this by myself   I held my breath and felt a storm gather   I
place a teacup in my palm, then between my teeth   The screen
goes dark   At night you thought it was morning   It will take
you half an hour to pack   The nurse tells me they are moving
you   but she doesn't know where   I'm pouring on houses,
a deluge wrecking gutters and pipes   There's no-one who needs
this much weather   This is a twister   In the centre I turn
Ringmaster, fire a pistol, tame rain, force thunder to stay in its
place   You tell me I can't cure the weather so I   sigh
out   ocean waves, write on the storm-clouds
with lightning   *I am on my way.*

Cause and Effect

i.

I whistled to the albatross, stabbed her with my pen, and she never called me back, changed all her numbers.

The gull's shit got in my eyes and I stumbled into his arms. He was all covered in guano and nitrogen; *think of the fertiliser,* he kept saying.

I gave a heron a lift to the coast in my convertible, spent a fortune, wined and dined him the best seafood. He had his mouth open for my pleasure.

The swan hung its neck back into its body at midday and its wings beat the earth's breath. It broke all our arms and every bit of furniture.

ii.

When my mother's legs stopped working and we waited for the social worker, a crow flew into the cracked conservatory. My sister ran to the kitchen – looking for an implement while I shut the French doors and stared at it, not letting it out of my sight. My father couldn't believe what a fuss we were making, said it came often to see him, to tell him the news.

The Relocation

There was once a god of mischief who sat
as the young men went to sea to find more land

that spring. He whispered to the daughters left to make
a house just for him, a house of disorder

and darkness that he could keep warm with fire.
April light fell in the soft places and he stood outside

in his flat cap. She, apron-clad, called the others,
all that was left of the village, to watch as the windows

of the house grew so large that only light survived.
The balance left the fjords that winter. They felt

the chime of trees tell them what to expect that season;
captured in moments, a memorial to planks of wood

and curtains, all the relics left by chaos. The tilt of change
to kill time, to mark all that's left and good about a place.

Ten Pieces of Driftwood

Resting

If I lie here a while, just touching your outer edges, lean
upon you, if you don't notice me touching, is that OK?

Dog-shaped

A dog carved by weather. My face
and my hand is splintered.

Distance

Can barely whisper, I wish you would lean on me
like you used to last year when you were free. I wish
I could see you better.

The woman in the window frame

The woman in the window hangs her rags
on red walls. In the house
nothing dries.

Erection

You didn't hold me up, I was going to that dishevelled hut
in the middle of the wood
anyway.

That man who used to shout downstairs

His nurse came to see us after one bad night, do you remember?
She told us he had a disease that made tiny noises sound loud
as thunder. We got drunk and danced, do you remember?

Animals

I have this rodent living inside
my guts, gnawing sharp teeth to the sounds of the forest.

Moss

The forest crumbles into peat and I could roll
green, push away the soft and stay there, all warm.

Exposure

When there is no door anymore, just rotten
frames, anyone can get in.

Soon everything will be trees

When wildflowers take over the earth, when moss
turns golden, when maps make no more sense
than the patterns swallows make, then everything
will be trees.

The Captain

I was sick today and took something I thought would improve
me but it didn't. I wanted a way to escape
to a place where I half-lived as a warning.
So I went to see my boss, in his office, full of slogans
and his rugby shirt, and the mug his kids bought for him.
He was kind and we didn't talk much, we talked
about boats. I listened to his tale of how he skippered
a yacht last weekend from Birling Gap to Dover.
I heard myself tell him how I learned to sail off the coast
of Kos. I realised I was good at taking orders.
Caught in a squall and I thought I'd die, I saw waves
a thousand feet high and the monsters…
He laughed gently and we knew boats do what they're told,
built to tilt and heel. I threw up
all the contents of the last few months. The day was overcast.
I was sick, caught in the jib, cut into the split
and falling sky. *Go home,* he said, *tie yourself to the mast.*

Prayer to be Said at Sea in a Storm

It knocks through my chest in its hunger to be owned by you,
what does that? To smash through myself and into your bed,
to see you sleep, or to be John Donne on a cliff top, flailing
at the wind, will you listen then? Play chess with me, play hide
and seek, make believe or simply sing to me. Maybe it's just that.
A sharp pitch of air: grows louder while you are not there.
Can I make you into a *thou*? Even if you don't want me,
I will carry my limbs and bones all over the world, making you
look, slipping into every one of your storms until it turns to laughter.
To make the world yours, I will be your breakwater, with fair winds
and following seas. I will be your wife if you will sail with me.

Davy Jones' Locker

i.

What is this stuff? Sediments of flesh at the bottom of the ocean. It takes time to decay. Her insides expand with gas. She floats like a ship, boarded by seabirds, seducing sharks. And all the sky gods look on, lick their lips.

ii.

I avoid Jonah, who follows me about the ship. I study my books. The skipper says that drowning's the worst death, like a million elephants sitting on your chest. He says he knows because he fell into a pond when he was six.

iii.

A giant octopus asks; *What're books*? Hindu goddess with all those arms; appears at the port side, brains in her fingertips, feels my pulse, pulls me down full fathoms five. I can't swim. I was ashamed when they fished me out, gasping for breath.

iv.

Lantern fish, blacksmelt, and hagfish live on the dead whale. A body glows in all the blood oil; with a sticky arm, snags food that glues to skin, turns to shell there. I saw her. There is nothing but honesty down there.

v.

Beached, fed on, a reef of shipwrecked wood. There's an art to being washed up. I share snippets of songs, the odd tall-tale, my glass eye, false teeth, vertebrae. There are two tons of carbon flux, no story goes to waste.

The Act of Slipping

It is a smart move to dive with the right equipment.
I still hear the stutter of reporters and photographers
that cold November morning when you waded up to your neck,
a blasted heart covered with a steel cylinder of diver's gas.
It was freezing cold and you drove so fast to catch the slack tide,
I still hear the sound of the mackerel.
I really miss you. I was there at the tideline,
shivering against a cold blast and that sound
of a motorbike backfiring against the hallowed, bright sky.

Sea Shanty

She pulls on sou'wester and galoshes
as god-soaked
choke of grey lashes the deck.

Some legend ties him to rocks
by his liver, tells him to stay there,
slaps every second he swallows

brine by the gallon. She ropes him,
knuckles taut, sees his eyes
flicker, reflect lightning

inside sky, his sea inside.
These are only stories she tells him
as he hefts onto the boat

and as the storm subsides.
He cooks her herring on the stove.
She picks bones

from her mouth, drinks down
rainwater and watches him
turn silver-grey, drop scales

from his tail, eyes always open
to the fish inside him.
They tell each other parables

of impossible sailing adventures,
sing songs of crazy beings
that went to sea in a sieve

and how, one day, they might
live happily ever after but miss
the smack and churn of ocean-spit.

No Place Like Home

She didn't want Angela Merkel to take our queen. She kept saying it over and over – that little woman from the village, clicking ruby slippers while I grumbled about petrol prices. She must have thought me stuck-up though nice enough to pass the time of day before the post office shut.

I drive in the pouring rain until I get to the coast and would have driven into the sea if I'd not run out of petrol. Wolf clouds mock me, tell me I've nothing here, no children, a failure, some kind of aberration. This is the wrong country.

I'd worn the wrong shoes, my father said, I've the wrong man living in my house, the wrong head, wrong country, wrong world on the wrong shoulders.

I went out on my own last night to a Korean restaurant, ordered the wrong thing again and everyone else's was better, there is a German word for that, I'm sure. I was given silver chopsticks by a girl with great hair. I felt like crying.

My sister phones and speaks to me like a stranger about our father. I want to tell her to see a shrink and hang up, but I say things will be fine. There's nonsense on the radio as I drive home. Later, I watch a documentary about the Inuit and how they have lost their rights to hunt whales. The ice is evaporating. For some people there is no place like home.

If John Clare was my Father

he might have taken me to look at what makes a land and person,
counted my metre by weather, held my hand as I stumbled from rocks

into spaces that he could understand. I might ask him where summer
comes from. Now, it arrives sure-footed as I slip into ditches and fissures.

Quarantined since March, this village retreats to where I am, with just
an hour's walk to see bluebells turn to the brightening light and blend

into a streak of flesh that withers to make way for wild garlic, fern,
then quaking grass, then soft rush. That's where I am, in the in-between

wildflower and weed, wedged in his words and this summer, my bold-
clothed god is in good mood because his dinner's just right, nothing yet smashed,

he sits, reclined, reading the ancient poets' tales of seasons, a courtly flourish
from a distant land, he can still taste its spice on the back of his tongue.

There is another voice in the sedge grass, a poor boy singing with words
as sharp as a violin, of a god that gives and takes. A man, a few doors down,

waves at me from his mother's house – where he's lived seventy years,
sleeps in the same bed where she bled into the streams of iron-rich springs.

I'm where the rocks break the breeze between hedges and verges and settles,
twists into the shape of our shadows, that's where I am. A place

where rivers force upwards, burst through in small wounds,
that's where I am. If John Clare was my father I would be home.

Wrecker

There are bags and dust, dust from bags and another life
landed in old suitcases that once cost you good money,
tight jammed with papers, clothes, letters from a child,
snagged cards from people that made you smile.
This paint's turned hard with age, I say, I decorated it
this way, but done nothing since he left, just lived and swam
about the house, tried not to wreck things.
Wanderers and exiles happen around me. Soul-flung,
jettisoned, stuffed in cupboards, you say that's all scuttle
and sink as I rummage in corners, to see what I can salvage.
There's banging on walls, a baby's yell. Life happens
in cracks and shouts, the marks etched in the wall,
that second of violence, a defiant scar to show I've gone
to ground, *perhaps I never had anything to lose.*

The Painter of Modern Life

I visit art galleries inside my television where the Chinese artist
smashes a house down, serves the people crab as a mark of respect,
a dissident joke we don't get in the West   I pretend to read
Baudelaire, my bookshelf – a delight these days, but admit to who
will care, I'm on Facebook and TikTok   The children; scared,
as I once was, throw charades of brave and fierce shapes   They
don't know what's new, lost or gained   I share the space and ask
the man I'm locked down with   *Back in the day when we wore
such beautiful clothes, were we stranger then or just the same?*   He
answers   *we no longer exist* and smeared with bleak extremes of
shame, listen to the street   clap and wring their hands   Now
the artist, man of the world and man of crowds are pixels made
of light and words   The papers aren't printed, and don't say
anything anyway   We watch the news every day, stare at death
on the television and I walk for an hour in an ever-growing careless
tide   The bluebells are wilder this year than ever   He's   so
busy piecing it together, in America, on YouTube   I try to tell
him about bluebells   I mute meetings in Zoom, pretend to be on
important calls   Crowds are no longer our domain. *I think it
will blow over*, I lie   He can't listen as I reach for Utopia, a new
Jerusalem where no one drinks or smokes   He says *What about
Africa? What about your family in India?*   My aunt sends flowers
on WhatsApp, *Show your father the Tulsi in our garden*   I report
back that he doesn't want to see them, or speak to anyone   My
sister says my mother's fallen — so far away   I tell her to call 111
and that helpline they set up at the council   WhatsApp blinks
in messages: *We went that time to Belur Math, in '73 after the
war, do you remember? Your father met a monk called Jithen who invited
us to eat with him, — my didi, your baby sister, your parents, my mother*

He blessed us because you were from England, how funny   *Ask*
your father   I send her a picture of the cherry blossom outside my
kitchen.   No, I don't remember   *Show your father*
the Tulsi in our garden, in England   *they call it holy basil.*   I want
to become a bluebell   The kids on TikTok make Big Macs, KFCs,
Nando's at home and we watch robots make love on TV   He's
dreamed it all before, he says   Perhaps he's Shiva, who dreams
of destruction   I've sent away for an effigy of a Norse god
I say little things make all the difference,   we change, a virus
changes   I see tigers in cages on Netflix but they're no longer tigers.

Ship's Cat

Seaboard in that tight-inch twitch of the ship,
struck by the pulleys, your high-tail flick is stuck
where the ship-in-a-bottle smacks an eighth life.

Hide in whorls of the deck, stow trapped with sows
and stags, an ark-full of creatures, unsure how
you got here through that tight bottleneck.

Tricks of oak flowers, broom, meadowsweet. Perch
on a driftwood girl marked with gold ink,
a carved figurehead, a chest to make men heel,

lap from her bowl and rigging. She'll hold the keel,
if the sky-sail fails, save your scrap-wood. This world
is driftwood, you're tied to a mast.

A twist of your collar bones, a spill of flesh laced
with vervain, fig and foxglove, and you wake in a car-park
as the shanty stops and this sea is gravel-hard.

The scuttled hulk set you free. You squeeze a ninth life
from a salvaged tank. Emerge near-drowned
in those middle years, escape the jar of painted sea.

Aliens

He loved those plain barren places, *Let's grow old by the sea,*
yearned for her dull light, cut-price clothes that glowed

by the light of the retirement homes, warden-controlled,
alarmed if needed. He remembers the way to the beach.

Old tunes heard through sandy suburbs, piped into beach huts
where they first met, like Britishers, strolling Cox's Bazar.

His accent made her laugh, thick as a sailor's. He doesn't want
to be one of those men who sit in arcades dressed like Elvis.

They wait on the chairs outside the cafe with a view of the moon.
She sits staring all day at the dust-bowl sea, asks *is it that time,*

is that time again please? The rattle of pills to quiet the breeze.
He's come far across dark water, there's still ash on the sand

where they burnt the ship. She is shrunk, dry and indrawn,
slaked in make-up, tattered jeans, leans on her frame,

calls in her moon-shivered voice to her once-shining sun,
your mother called you after the red morning light. He nods

and they change into their original shapes for a moment.
A waitress arrives at last, *so sorry, it gets busy this time of night.*

Mumbles Head

A cyclist's bell yells alarm. A boy tugs on his father for a show of love. You talk
rubbish to help the deluge, listen with your best face. Bright with admiration.

What's good about the one-sided conversation is unspoken. Constructed, it helps
to talk. After the walk, you sit in a crumbling room together to understand

what happened in the last century. Eliot and Pound thought we shouldn't be
so sincere. *I've never been to Cox's Bazar. Someone told me it's full of refugees now.*

When your sister made tea just like your broken mother, desperate *shall I heat up
the curry?* You reddened and burned. Bengali by heritage. Fish, scales and tails.

Sit down, sister, and *she isn't feeding.* Your father shouts at the social worker
to leave them alone, makes paneer with old pans. Will they help anyway?

Love's messenger. There was a lot of paperwork he had to do to get out of
paying. The phone a weapon. To speak is to bleed. The *'my'* takes your place

in the family, and they relax. Anybody would quickly get help for you. Temperate
brightness of sun. Jet-ski in the harbour. Ferries push on towards Pembroke docks,

don't worry about us. The rocks misshapen as mould, a decay. Uncles turned ash.
Your mother keeps asking to be taken to hospital, *Let's go now.* No one is going

to take her this weekend, you tell her. The woman mouths words in another
language. Drawing out memory for ramshackle pasts. You potter and look.

Potter and look. Can anything be done? His food is better than any take-away.
He still eats the fish from the 'Eye of Bengal' and complains about the weather

in this country. He talks about the next stage of the EU negotiations and how
Wales will never be free of England. He says Wales has cut itself with a knife.

He talks about climate change and how they will grow chickpeas in Norfolk
and this will be good. Less air miles for food. At night you stay in a cheap hotel.

Sand covers your bed and there are no sheets. You sleep in the thighs of the tide.
You dream about Sylvia Plath. The cars and the waves become one noise.

You ignore them both. You think you know too much about the sex lives of insects
but not about poets. There is no wi-fi code. You explain why people voted to leave

to your sister over breakfast. She already knows. You blame her for things, they put
beans on your plate. You blame her for that. You look out at Mumbles Head.

What brought you to this tourist village in the tail-end of Autumn when there are
no people you remember from your past who are ready to hold you?

Have you been lost? When you walk past the playing fields of your infant school
why do you wave? It seems so clean to you these days.

They seem to have the recycling under control. You only use the bathroom once
on your visit as you think it smells. You are ambivalent about 'climate change'

as you know you will die. You think you will die soon and your breath burns
and your teeth hurt, there are no children or grandchildren. You know an awful lot

about human evolution and very little about breast milk. You think about
pop culture and bands you liked, wonder where all your books on Bowie went.

He's talking about Cox's Bazar again and how it reminds him of Mumbles Head.
He is watching the news on his iPad and ignoring you. You are glad.

Baba, thumi kitchu bhala lagi? Amar ma ekene thaki na. You don't know how to say
anything. They don't know how else to live. The Welsh women stood

on Mumbles Head, prayed for all their boys and men. The waves have always
been the waves. She says the coast always looks the same, wherever you are.

Windfall

I imagine standing next to the carcass – *poor, poor creature* –
with an urge to hold it, when it's time.
Off it goes into its next adventure. Blubber and bone.
A flicker of an amulet from that shaman catches
the light around your neck. *I love everything about you.*
Close to the end; you come into sharp focus. Bodies built
to withstand waves of birth and death and the blackfish
swimming in our chests. *Let it go.* She was a matriarch.
Probably died of old age. The shoals were rich
the last four summers. She'd been seen chasing herring.
Her teeth were worn. *Let go of time.*
Floki sent ravens from the Faroe Islands to look for food
and a place to rest. They found a windfall washed up
on that new shore. It fed his wife for two years.

Father's Day

My father; torn sofa, worn cushions piled high,
didn't teach me to swim when I was a child.
Me; accusing over breakfast, that day the world
was hot; *you made my life harder. Some children cry
for their mothers.* At that poolside; his own head
submerged again remembering dusk in a Bengal pond,
he was only reaching for dragonflies – as boys do,

falling under. He was always talking about those ponds.
He took me, crying, to a library, safety in silence,
hope laid out in front of me, a magician's set of books.
Stay safe on an island, or stacked on shelves,
and later we watched those fantasy films, with gorgons,
hydra, harpies, *look* he said – *look what creatures
are in the world.* I yelled *It's camera trick*s, proud to dispel

his myths and we laughed. Last month he began
to cook again for his bedridden wife, like he did
thirty years ago, that first time she was taken to hospital,
her voices threatening to poison us.
Last month, on a cursory visit on my sister's insistence,
I noticed he hadn't cleaned the house. *It's an illusion –*
he told me – *I won't bother because the dirt always returns.*

Reading the Upanishads, he sits in his priority seat
in the living room, the only place where you can see
the TV, where he ignores the world,
even though he wants to live to see it drown
and watch all the creatures sink into the earth. Today
it's Father's Day – I've sent no card to say *thank you
for what you did and didn't do.*

Whale Watching

They say that there was a body. That his hands
had turned into fins well before the last ice age.
He had a heart the size of Scotland
and his tail fluke could smash the whole of the coast
to sand. His tongue washed up on the Thames
one summer. I was taking a course on Renaissance
painting at the National Gallery. They said I should go
and find him; study his body for what it means.
They say he had a wife but lost her long before
the Old Testament was written. She was a tree,
they said. I sailed around Glamorgan, Land's End,
Portsmouth, survived all the Shipping Forecast,
the news of losing identities at the forties.
They say: *make him look magnificent. Paint his eyes
with whale fat,* the stuff Turner used to paint skies.
I never got to see him. They said he was stuffed full
of plastic and petroleum. *It's enough to worship art,
the body of god is just a foolish allegory.* When I returned
to shore, my overalls were covered in his spume.

Banshee

When I opened my mouth to sing, he shook his head,
It's feathered, that's true but it's no birdsong.

When I opened my mouth to sing, they sighed,
There she goes again, too bold, too wide of the mark.

When I opened my legs to sing, the whole universe
sailed in and out of the sluice gates to my surprise.

When I opened my mouth to sing, all the pheasants, parrots, peacocks,
cuckoos, hens, and gulls wept. They'd never heard such beautiful music.

Asylum

She's remembered – from her handful of shattered bones,
a weather's wind scattering her cards to give answers.

How she has suffered with those she saw suffer – over
and over – those documentary films twisting their words,

keeping books close, revealing all her father's secrets
and people listen, pride themselves with an ear for stories.

Alone on the beach as the tide scatters her remnants,
the wind writes back in cursive and sand like Sanskrit,

tells her sometimes things change in a shock of ways,
wolves turn porpoise, bears turn walrus, elephants turn whale.

Her bones, her battered body, left dismembered
and she's right here, in front of a TV watching commentaries.

When the remembering happens, the shaman sits in an old
church near Kew Gardens, dust blown in her eyes

from a humid and unstable sea. She turns over his answers,
all those stuck records, and she's still here – by his side.

She is looking for fathers who force nature to do things
it shouldn't and the answers he gives say nothing

but *keep asking for help*. Once she held daffodils and played
in a snow-laden garden, fell on her birthday, painted

her face like her mother's, danced and prowled fierce
like a snow-leopard. How full of wonder she was then.

Her friend calls from an island, talks about energy,
paradigms melting, shifting sands, she's learning to play,

and has so many lovers. *Who will tell my stories when I'm gone?*
She asks her friend, who replies she has too many to tell.

All life will flow when the tide decides, built from a swell
of butterflies that can hear the heartbeat of gazelles running

into the perimeter fence of a national park. She asks the cards
if she can turn them around. Her father's books on the earth

were pessimistic, graphs were off the scale. She phones her father
for help with equations. He's watching the flood on a small screen.

He knew of the stranding from the start, yet still fathered her,
always muttering *it's too late; it's already happened* – the wave

is on us, teachable moments. He shows her how to fall
into the sea, turn whale, be remembered by small acts of magic.

The Unreliable Memoirs of the
Unsinkable Molly Brown

I met a deep-sea diver with a fear of water, who held secrets.
She knew I couldn't swim, said *start small, take a hot bath, feel
your body expand, loose its shape.* These are first steps to bravery.

I met a Swedish girl who held me in her generous hands
on the rocks in Stenkusten, while I was slippery-footed and unsure,
and we swam together in a whirlpool she found for me.

I met a boy I loved with a broad back, he knew I had a fear
of drowning. He took me to Berlin to swim in the Liquidrom
and the Badeschiff. *You can't sink,* he told me, as I climbed on board.

I'd no idea how I met the ice-cold sea, through gaps and blanks
where the seeping crept, and no time to think or read the papers.
I was so-so prepared, no time for graphs or PowerPoint.

It's amazing what you can muster when you are terrified. I met
my body, all brined and salted, made of icebergs and disaster.

The Caller

There is a legend that I was once from India
before the world was so broken and left scraps
of me here in the kitchen. I throw the night door open,
listening for him. Somewhere behind the fox call,
there is laughter, a rattle, fly-catcher, over here,
his tight trick and urgent call ticks from his guts.

Come here, come here. Night singer,
I didn't hear over the noises; the television, the cooker,
next-door's moans. I'm leaning from the window
as he reaches quietly at first, and can I answer
I'm here, at last, ready to duet, into a blank
and deadly future. There is a legend that nightingales

sang for the Indian Kings. Can I entice him
with the smells of spice? I shed these fake leopard-skin
slippers and run into the garden, Ovid-charmed,
alarm-called, sprout-beak and shrink-eye.
I grow lung-song sharp and he keeps calling,
come, come, and my human hunger is marked

for his words to sing our lonely songs
from a kitchen window forever in the dead of dark.
Fly-catcher, rattler, all my island's voices, *call again,*
and my brown feathers appear for a moment
as he sings more urgently, now night-jar, windfallen
in the coal dark. *Come here, come here.*

Notes

Notes from a Shipwreck: The phrase *Salus populi suprema lex esto* (<u>Latin</u>: "The health (welfare, good, salvation, felicity) of the people should be the supreme law", "Let the good (or safety) of the people be the supreme (or highest) law" or "The welfare of the people shall be the supreme law") is a maxim or principle found in Cicero's *De Legibus* (book III, part III, sub. VIII). Quoted by Boris Johnson during Covid 19 lockdown, 2020.

A young Minke Whale died near Barnes Bridge in southwest London in May 2021 after getting separated from its mother. It was put down by vets around the 11th May. Flowers were placed on it by onlookers. Minke whales are the smallest of the Great Whales. Vets from London Zoo reported that they couldn't rule out man-made climate change for increasing numbers of cetaceans stranded in the Thames.

Outcaste: **Badmash** – Hindi: rogue, naughty person. **Brahmin**: In the Hindu caste system, the Brahmin (or Priest) caste is at the top, followed by Kshatriya (Rulers), Vaishyas (Merchants) Shudras (workers) and outside this – the Dalits (Outcastes). The system was in place from before 1000 BCE. Recent research shows that before the 18th century and the onset of the British Raj, the caste system was relatively flexible but after British rule it became far more rigid. After independence, discrimination based on caste was outlawed. However, there is still a struggle to create parity of opportunity based on caste. **The Howrah Bridge** crosses the Hoogley River in Kolkata. **The War**: The Bangladesh war of independence, 1972 (fought and won against West Pakistan). **The Dharmasutras** are Hindu texts dating back to 2nd millennium BCE to the early centuries of the 1st millennium BCE. They contain rules and guides for law and how to live. They are contradictory and leave a lot to interpretation. One of the edicts is that Hindus must not cross the sea (or Black Water) or they will loose their caste and religion.

The Shipboard Girl: This poem is inspired by the artwork *The Shipboard Girl* by Roy Lichtenstein.

Caliban: **Lark's Head:** A knot – sometimes used in making fishing nets.

The Portent: **Comet West** was one of the brightest objects in the sky in 1976 and went largely unreported due to the disappointment caused by the expectations of Comet Kahoutek in 1973.

Eating with Hands: Eating with hands is a custom in many countries. In Indian cultures it is said to originate within Ayurvedic teachings. The Vedic people believed that bodies synchronised with the elements of nature and that hands hold power. The rhyme about the fingers relates to Ayurvedic texts which teach that each finger is an extension of one of the five elements.

Black Water Shanty: Black Water is a reference to Hindu term for 'Ocean'. The poem is inspired by Arthur Rimbaud's *The Drunken Boat.*

Tethys is a Greek goddess. Originally Oceanus' consort. In Hellenistic and Roman poetry, Tethys' name came to be used as a poetic term for the sea. She plays very little part in Greek mythology and is mainly forgotten.

Sea Voices: **Lascar** is a Portuguese term for sailor and used by the East India Company. Due to the high sickness rates in British sailors travelling to India, high numbers of sailors were recruited from Bengal and Assam. The name *lascar* was also used to refer to Indian servants, typically engaged by British military officers. **Sepoy**: means infantry man or soldier. In the Bengal Army, sepoys were often recruited from 'high' caste Hindu families unlike other parts of the army. Often whole villages and families would be recruited together in a platoon to serve the British Army. **Mir Zafar:** A controversial figure in Indian and Bangladeshi history as the first 'puppet' ruler (Nawab) for the East India Company and a symbol of intimate betrayal and treachery among many Indians, Pakistanis and Bangladeshis.

The Tower of London: Before the zoo opened in Regent's Park, many 'gifts' of tigers, lions and other animals from all over the British Empire were kept at the Tower of London. **Black Water:** Due to the Brahmins' forbidding *'crossing the black water'*, many sailors in the East India Company and British Navy had to travel over land by foot which led to many deaths.

When God Visits Me He is Covered In Glitter: **Satori** is a Zen Buddhist concept of awakening or enlightenment.

Professor of Primates: **Altruism** is the a term in evolutionary biology where the organism forgoes its own *fitness* in order to benefit another organism or *community*. Biological *fitness* refers to the ability of the organism to leave viable offspring. Many argue that seemingly altruistic acts are really kin-selection (benefiting the genes of relatives) or just a way of getting sex (mating behaviours). **Lar, Hoolock, Siamang**: Species of Gibbons. They sing to each other for mating and warnings. This poem is dedicated to Professor Volker Sommer who has taught human evolution and primatology to various primates (including me) during his long career at UCL. He is a respected authority on many primates including Gibbons. He is also known for his conservation and field work.

The Slip is a term for a vessel being lowered safety into the water and also refers to a boat's 'parking space'. **Abort point:** is the final point at which a ship can take action to avoid passing the point of no return. **Hardtack**: ship's biscuits/rations.

Anchorage is a place of safety where a vessel can drop anchor. **Kasper Hauser:** A person who turned up in Nuremberg in 1828 with a note saying he had been in isolation all his life. He became a minor celebrity. He is the subject of films, books and poems; notably the film *The Enigma of Kasper Hauser* (1973) by Werner Herzog, which is referred to in the poem.

And the Harbourmaster Says: **Harbourmaster**: The most senior official who is in charge of a port and everyone in or near the port's safety. Harbourmaster's words are collaged from fragments of the UK National Shipbuilding Strategy, 2017 (MOD). **The Ghost:** Shipbuilding was a hazardous occupation and deaths were a daily occurrence, creating the rise of trade unions and by the end of the 1960s, safety committees existed in most yards. With the introduction of the Health and Safety at Work Act 1974, accident rates were greatly reduced.

Overboard: **meds:** medication. **bitter end:** The Bitt is the post that the rope on a ship is fastened to. The last piece of rope let out is the 'bitter end'. **Silent Period:** the point just after an SOS has been sent when a boat is in danger. **Spin**: Thorough search of a cell or room.

Hungry Ghost: in many eastern cultures **Hungry Ghost** refers to a spirit that will not rest (often residing inside a person). In Hindu culture it is termed Preta and is fed rice so it can reincarnate.

Dazzle Ship camouflage (also known as Razzle Dazzle or Dazzle painting) was a military camouflage paint-scheme used on ships during World War I and II. The idea is credited to the artist Norman Wilkinson, used to disrupt vision, and a forerunner of modern pop art design.

Long Glass refers to a ship's telescope.

Wrecker is a smuggling term for the people who would light beacons on dangerous cliffs in a storm to pretend to be lighthouses and so causing shipwrecks in order to loot the ship's cargo.

If John Clare Was My Father: This poem was written in 2020 as a commission from poet Adam Horovitz for the podcast The Thunder Mutters celebrating the 200th anniversary of the publication of Clare's debut collection *Poems Descriptive of Rural Life and Scenery.*

Painter of Modern Life: 'The Painter of Modern Life' is an 1863 essay by Charles Baudelaire. It is a manifesto of modernity and asks what art is in relationship to modern culture. **Tigers on Netflix**: *Tiger King* was a popular true-crime documentary aired during 2020 about the criminal treatment of wild animals in the USA and propelled Joe Exotic to stardom.

Aliens: This poem was inspired by the project of poet Suzannah V. Evans who asked me to respond to Jules Laforgue's 'Complainte de la lune en province'. My poem is in no way a 'translation' but is inspired by a reading of this and his other 'moon' poems.

Mumbles Head: **Cox's Bazar** is the most famous beach and tourist town in Bangladesh. Thousands of terrified Rohingya refugees began arriving onto the beaches and paddy fields of southern Bangladesh in August 2017, 60% were children. By August 2021 there were 800,000 refugees – making it now one of the largest refugee camps in the world. **Eye of Bengal:** generic name for an Indian restaurant. **Belur Math:** a Temple in Kolkata. **Didi:** sister. **"Baba.."** *translates to "Dad, do you like anything? My mother is no longer here"* **Mumbles Head**: rocky headland on the coast of Swansea.

Floki, son of Vilgerd, is mentioned in the Viking Sagas *Landnámabók* (*The Book of Settlements*) and legend says he voyaged into the unknown and discovered the Faroe Islands and Iceland. **Windfall**: term for washed up whales, also Drift Whale.

The Unreliable Memoirs of the Unsinkable Molly Brown: **Molly Brown** was a philanthropist, activist, and was one of the survivors of The Titanic, and the subject of a musical called *The Unsinkable Molly Brown*.

Acknowledgements and Thanks

Thanks to all the editors of journals that have published versions of poems in this collection:

Poetry Birmingham Literary Journal, 14, Tears in the Fence, Under the Radar, Riggwelter, Molly Bloom, Finished Creatures, Pippa Ran Books, High Window, Poetry Wales, Ink, Sweat & Tears, Agenda, Bare Fiction, Anthropocene, The Journal, Broken Sleep Books and *Magma*.

Thanks to Suzannah V. Evans for introducing me to Jules Laforgue. Thanks to the many teachers, mentors, poets and poetry groups who have supported and inspired my work over the last few years – notably Patricia McCarthy, Sandeep Parmar, Jan Heritage, Mimi Khalvati, Julia Webb and Jemma Borg. Enormous thanks to Nine Arches Press, Jane Commane for her skill, kindness and patient insight into editing this work and Angela Hicken for support.

This work would not exist without the friends who inspired me to write about ships; Gareth (RIP), Simon, Jo & Paul on that very first ship. To Cathy & Madhu, Jad & Julie and to all my family and friends who have kept me afloat over the years.